"Using Pointers in Java

VOLUME 2

Pointer ptr=null;

j POINTER

- Efficient Memory Management
- Much Better Time Complexity
- No Security Flaws

Aatif Ahmad Khan

PREFACE

Based on the feedback on Volume 1 of this book and to add many more new things to 'Using Pointers in Java', am releasing the Volume 2 of it.

Volume 2 includes a complete implementation of Singly Linked List along with usefulness of Pointers in Java. Advantages are discussed in detail. To give a full proof of advantages, snapshots of end results are also included.

Code snippets are given in form of snapshots taken from NetBeans Java IDE.

Suggestions from my readers are most welcome.

You may mail me feedback and suggestions at pointersinjava@gmail.com

                                                    Aatif Ahmad Khan

ACKNOWLEDGEMENT

First of all, I thank my Lord ALLAH (paak), without whom writing this book is not possible.

I am also thankful to my college mentor Ms. Shweta Singhal for her suggestions on the usefulness and advantages of Pointers in Java.

I am also thankful to website http://www.stackoverflow.com for the introductory knowledge which proved to be extremely useful in this project.

I must also thank CreateSpace for their publishing services.

Aatif Ahmad Khan

INDEX

1. INTRODUCTION

A pointer is a special kind of variable that holds the address of another variable.

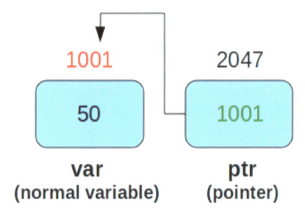

Figure 1: Basic definition of a Pointer

"Java has a Pointer model that eliminates the possibility of overwriting memory and corrupting data." [1]

Unlike C/C++, Pointer Model of Java is not freely accessible to users. But for developers, there is still some scope to access Pointers using Unsafe class in sun.misc package [2]

'Using Pointers in Java' is an attempt to utilize the power of Pointers in Java freely but securely. To maintain the security, Exception Handling is used primarily.

So let us firstly define our Pointer class as:

```
Pointer.java  ×

Source  History

1    package am.aatif;
2    /**
3     *
4     * @author Aatif Ahmad Khan
5     */
6    public class Pointer {
7        public static long address;
8    }
9
```

Figure 2: Code for Pointer class declaration

2. THE GETUNSAFE() METHOD

To utilize the Unsafe class we must instantiate it using getUnsafe() method [3]

```java
public Unsafe getUnsafe()
{
    boolean oh=false;
    Unsafe unsafe=null;
    try
    {
        Field f = Unsafe.class.getDeclaredField("theUnsafe");
        f.setAccessible(true);
        oh=true;
        unsafe=(Unsafe)f.get(null);
    }
    catch(Exception ex)
    {
        System.out.println("Exception: "+ex);
    }
    if(oh==false)
    {
        return null;
    }
    else
    {
        return unsafe;
    }
}
```

Figure 3: Code for getUnsafe() method

Once Unsafe class is instantiated we could use following methods [4] :

- *allocateMemory(long bytes)*: to allocate bytes
- *putInt(long address, int i)*: to put an int i at address location
- *getInt(long address)*: to get an int for location address

To make this project **Compiler Unspecific** [5], following data members are used:

- *Integer.SIZE*
- *Long.SIZE*

3. GETTING MEMORY ADDRESS

Now let us see how to get memory address of a variable:

```java
package address;
/**
 * @Author Aatif Ahmad Khan
 */

import java.lang.reflect.Field;
import sun.misc.Unsafe;

public class Address {
    public static void main(String[] args) {
        Unsafe unsafe=getUnsafe();
        long address=unsafe.allocateMemory(Integer.SIZE);
        unsafe.putInt(address, 5);
        System.out.println("Integer 5 placed at address: "+address);
    }
```

Figure 4 & 5: Getting memory address of a variable

```java
    public static Unsafe getUnsafe()
    {
        boolean oh=false;
        Unsafe unsafe=null;
        try
        {
            Field f = Unsafe.class.getDeclaredField("theUnsafe");
            f.setAccessible(true);
            oh=true;
            unsafe=(Unsafe)f.get(null);
        }
        catch(Exception ex)
        {
            System.out.println("Exception: "+ex);
        }
        if(oh==false)
        {
            return null;
        }
        else
        {
            return unsafe;
        }
    }
}
```

```
Output - Address (run)
▷▷  run:
▷▷  Integer 5 placed at address: 413528048
    BUILD SUCCESSFUL (total time: 1 second)
```

Figure 6: Output for Getting memory address of a variable

Now let us use getUnsafe() Method, to place an int value to a user-allocated memory location:

```
class A{

    public static void main(String args){

        Unsafe unsafe=getUnsafe();

        long
    address=unsafe.allocateMemory(Integer.SIZE);

        unsafe.putInt(address, 4);

        System.out.println(unsafe.getInt(address));

    }

}
//Output:   4
```

Figure 7: Placing int value 4 to a user−allocated location

4. IMPLEMENTATION OF SINGLY LINKED LIST

Implementation of Linked List using Pointers in Java

//Code

Let us firstly implement Pointer class as shown in Figure 1.

```java
package am.aatif;
class Pointer{
    public static long address;
}
```

Figure 8: Declaration of Pointer class

field **address** is for storing the address of variable it is pointing to.

Next let us implement Node class as:

```java
package am.aatif;
import java.lang.reflect.Field;
import sun.misc.Unsafe;
/**
 *
 * @author Aatif Ahmad Khan
 */
public class Node {
    public static Pointer next;
    public static Pointer newNode(int k)
    {
        Unsafe u=getUnsafe();
        long add=u.allocateMemory(Integer.SIZE+Long.SIZE);
        u.putInt(add, k);
        u.putLong(add+Integer.SIZE, 0);
        next.address=add;
        return next;
    }
```

Figure 9: Code for Node class implementation

In Node class, we have defined an instance of Unsafe class.

Now Node is defined as follows

Figure 10: Pictorial representation of a Node

```
Node.java  x

Source  History

17          return next;
18     }
19     public static Unsafe getUnsafe()
20     {
21          boolean oh=false;
22          Unsafe unsafe=null;
23          try
24          {
25              Field f = Unsafe.class.getDeclaredField("theUnsafe");
26              f.setAccessible(true);
27              oh=true;
28              unsafe=(Unsafe)f.get(null);
29          }
           catch(Exception ex)
31          {
32              System.out.println("Exception: "+ex);
33          }
34          if(oh==false)
35          {
36              return null;
37          }
38          else
39          {
40              return unsafe;
41          }
42     }
43  }
44
```

Figure 11: Code for Node class implementation (Continued⋯)

We have returned a reference to this node.

Now let us implement the LinkedList class:

```java
package am.aatif;
import java.lang.reflect.Field;
import sun.misc.Unsafe;
import am.aatif.Node;
import am.aatif.Pointer;
/**
 *
 * @author Aatif Ahmad Khan
 */
public class LinkedList {
    long init;
    int count=0;
    long prev;
    void add(int k)
    {
        Unsafe unsafe=getUnsafe();
        if(count==0)
        {
            Pointer ptr=Node.newNode(k);
            init=ptr.address;
            prev=init;
        }
        else if(count==1)
        {
            Pointer ptr=Node.newNode(k);
            unsafe.putLong(init+Integer.SIZE, ptr.address);
            prev=ptr.address;
        }
```

Figure 12: Code for LinkedList class implementation

In this class, we have used two methods:

void add(int k): to add a node to LinkedList

void traverse(): to traverse the LinkedList and print the contents of nodes added to it

We have also used a variable count to count the number of nodes in List.

int count;

```
             prev=ptr.address;
28           }
29           else
30           {
31               Pointer ptr=Node.newNode(k);
                 unsafe.putLong(prev+Integer.SIZE, ptr.address);
                 prev=ptr.address;
34           }
35           count++;
36       }
37   void traverse()
38   {
39       if(count==0)
40       {
41           System.out.println("List contains 0 Elements!");
42       }
43       else
44       {
45           Unsafe u=getUnsafe();
46           System.out.print(u.getInt(init));
47           long nextAddress=(u.getLong(init+Integer.SIZE));
48           while(nextAddress!=0)
49           {
50               System.out.print(" -> "+u.getInt(nextAddress));
51               nextAddress=(u.getLong(nextAddress+Integer.SIZE));
52           }
53       }
54   }
```

Figure 13: Code for LinkedList class implementation (Continued⋯)

Now in the main() method we have added five elements 0, 1, 2, 3, 4 to the LinkedList ll:

Output is also shown in the next snapshot:

```
51            nextAddress=(u.getLong(nextAddress+Integer.SIZE));
52          }
53        }
54      }
55 ⊟   public static void main(String[] args) {
56        LinkedList ll=new LinkedList();
57        for(int k=0; k<5; k++)
58        {
59            ll.add(k);
60        }
61        ll.traverse();
62      }
```

Output - Pointer (run) x

```
run:
0 -> 1 -> 2 -> 3 -> 4BUILD SUCCESSFUL (total time: 0 seconds)
```

Figure 14: Code for main() method along with output

```
61            ll.traverse();
62      }
63      public Unsafe getUnsafe()
64 ⊟   {
65        boolean oh=false;
66        Unsafe unsafe=null;
67        try
68        {
69            Field f = Unsafe.class.getDeclaredField("theUnsafe");
70            f.setAccessible(true);
71            oh=true;
72            unsafe=(Unsafe)f.get(null);
73        }
       catch(Exception ex)
75        {
76            System.out.println("Exception: "+ex);
77        }
78        if(oh==false)
79        {
80            return null;
81        }
82        else
83        {
84            return unsafe;
85        }
86      }
87  }
```

Figure 15: Code for LinkedList class implementation (Continued⋯)

5. TIME COMPLEXITY ANALYSIS

We know that java.util package of Java Library has a LinkedList Implementation in class java.util.LinkedList.

Now let us compare the time complexity of Simple Implementation of LinkedList vs the implementation of LinkedList using Pointers in Java.

```java
package test;
import java.util.LinkedList;
/**
 *
 * @author Aatif Ahmad Khan
 */
public class Test {
    public static void main(String[] args) {
        LinkedList ll=new LinkedList();
        for(int k=0; k<500000; k++)
        {
            ll.add(k);
        }
        for(int k=0; k<500000; k++)
        {
            System.out.print(ll.get(k));
        }
    }
}
```

Figure 16: Code for Test class implementation

Results:

Table 1: Comparison of efficiency of Pointer's code with predefined Java Linked List code

Elements added (n)	t (Pointers)	t (Simple)
100000	2 seconds	18 seconds
200000	4 seconds	76 seconds
500000	10 seconds	528 seconds
1000000	19 seconds	2254 seconds
10000000	190 seconds	~66 hours

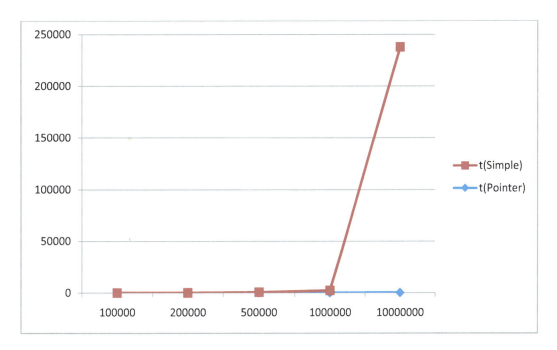

Figure 17: Line graph showing comparison results

Mathematical Interpretation:

Let t_0 be time required for adding 100000 elements to Linked list.

t_0 (Pointer Implementation) = 2 seconds

t_0 (Predefined Implementation) = 18 seconds

Now let k be the multiplying factor to the number of elements.

Then for Pointer's Implementation, equation comes out to be,

$$t(k \times n) = k \times t_0$$

And for Simple implementation, equation comes out to be,

$$t(k \times n) = k^2 \times t_0$$

These equations depict the efficiency of Pointer's implementation over Simple implementation.

Result Snapshots:

```
41          }
42          else
43          {
44              Unsafe u=getUnsafe();
45              System.out.print(u.getInt(init));
46              long nextAddress=(u.getLong(init+Integer.SIZE));
47              while(nextAddress!=0)
48              {
49                  System.out.print(" -> "+u.getInt(nextAddress));
50                  nextAddress=(u.getLong(nextAddress+Integer.SIZE));
51              }
52          }
53      }
54      public static void main(String[] args) {
55          LinkedList ll=new LinkedList();
56          for(int k=0; k<100000; k++)
57          {
58              ll.add(k);
59          }
60          ll.traverse();
61      }
```

Output - Pointer (run) x

```
9924 -> 99925 -> 99926 -> 99927 -> 99928 -> 99929 -> 99930 -> 99931 -> 99932 -> 99933 -> 99934 -> 99935 ->
99936 -> 99937 -> 99938 -> 99939 -> 99940 -> 99941 -> 99942 -> 99943 -> 99944 -> 99945 -> 99946 -> 99947 ->
 99948 -> 99949 -> 99950 -> 99951 -> 99952 -> 99953 -> 99954 -> 99955 -> 99956 -> 99957 -> 99958 -> 99959 -
> 99960 -> 99961 -> 99962 -> 99963 -> 99964 -> 99965 -> 99966 -> 99967 -> 99968 -> 99969 -> 99970 -> 99971
-> 99972 -> 99973 -> 99974 -> 99975 -> 99976 -> 99977 -> 99978 -> 99979 -> 99980 -> 99981 -> 99982 -> 99983
 -> 99984 -> 99985 -> 99986 -> 99987 -> 99988 -> 99989 -> 99990 -> 99991 -> 99992 -> 99993 -> 99994 -> 9999
5 -> 99996 -> 99997 -> 99998 -> 99999BUILD SUCCESSFUL (total time: 2 seconds)
```

Figure 18: Output for Pointer's Code with n=100000

Now testing same thing with Simple Implementation...

In Output numbers 1...99999 are printed as output instead of 1 -> 2...->99999

```
1    package test;
2    import java.util.LinkedList;
3
4
5     * @author Buenra
6     */
7    public class Test {
8        public static void main(String[] args) {
9            LinkedList ll=new LinkedList();
10           for(int k=0; k<100000; k++)
11           {
12               ll.add(k);
13           }
14           for(int k=0; k<100000; k++)
15           {
16               System.out.print(ll.get(k));
17           }
18       }
```

Output - Test (run) x

```
98709987199872998739987499875998769987799878998799988099881998829988399884998859988699887998889988999890998
91998929989399894998959989699897998989989999990099901999029990399904999059990699907999089990999910999119991 2
999139991499915999169991799918999199992099921999229992399924999259992699927999289992999993099931999329993399
93499935999369993799938999939999409994199942999439994499945999469994799948999499995099951999529995399954999 5
59995699957999589995999960999619996299963999649996599966999679996899969997099971999729997399974999759994769
99779997899979999809998199982999839998499985999869998799988999899999909999199992999939999499995999969999799 9
9899999BUILD SUCCESSFUL (total time: 18 seconds)
```

Figure 19: Output for Predefined Code with n=100000

```
41              }
42          else
43          {
44              Unsafe u=getUnsafe();
45              System.out.print(u.getInt(init));
46              long nextAddress=(u.getLong(init+Integer.SIZE));
47              while(nextAddress!=0)
48              {
49                  System.out.print(" -> "+u.getInt(nextAddress));
50                  nextAddress=(u.getLong(nextAddress+Integer.SIZE));
51              }
52          }
53      }
54      public static void main(String[] args) {
55          LinkedList ll=new LinkedList();
56          for(int k=0; k<1000000; k++)
57          {
58              ll.add(k);
59          }
60          ll.traverse();
61      }
```

```
Output - Pointer (run)  x

99930 -> 999931 -> 999932 -> 999933 -> 999934 -> 999935 -> 999936 -> 999937 -> 999938 -> 999939 -> 999940 -
> 999941 -> 999942 -> 999943 -> 999944 -> 999945 -> 999946 -> 999947 -> 999948 -> 999949 -> 999950 -> 99995
1 -> 999952 -> 999953 -> 999954 -> 999955 -> 999956 -> 999957 -> 999958 -> 999959 -> 999960 -> 999961 -> 99
9962 -> 999963 -> 999964 -> 999965 -> 999966 -> 999967 -> 999968 -> 999969 -> 999970 -> 999971 -> 999972 ->
999973 -> 999974 -> 999975 -> 999976 -> 999977 -> 999978 -> 999979 -> 999980 -> 999981 -> 999982 -> 999983
-> 999984 -> 999985 -> 999986 -> 999987 -> 999988 -> 999989 -> 999990 -> 999991 -> 999992 -> 999993 -> 999
994 -> 999995 -> 999996 -> 999997 -> 999998 -> 999999BUILD SUCCESSFUL (total time: 19 seconds)
```

Figure 20: Output for Pointer's Code with n=1000000

```
1    package test;
2    import java.util.LinkedList;
3
4
5     * @author Bushra
6
7    public class Test {
8        public static void main(String[] args) {
9            LinkedList ll=new LinkedList();
10           for(int k=0; k<1000000; k++)
11           {
12               ll.add(k);
13           }
14           for(int k=0; k<1000000; k++)
15           {
16               System.out.print(ll.get(k));
17           }
18       }
```

Output - Test (run) ×

```
999897999898999899999900999901999902999903999904999905999906999907999908999909999910999911999912999913999
991499991599991699991799991899991999992099992199992299992399992499992599992699992799992899992999993099999
319999329999339999349999359999369999379999389999399999409999419999429999439999449999459999469999479999489
999949999950999951999952999953999954999955999956999957999958999959999960999961999962999963999964999965999
996699996799996899996999997099997199997299997399997499997599997699997799997899997999998099998199998299999
839999849999859999869999879999889999899999909999919999929999939999949999959999969999979999989999999BUILD
SUCCESSFUL (total time: 37 minutes 34 seconds)
```

Figure 21: Output for Predefined Code with n=1000000

And the last one with n=10000000

```
41          }
42          else
43          {
44              Unsafe u=getUnsafe();
45              System.out.print(u.getInt(init));
46              long nextAddress=(u.getLong(init+Integer.SIZE));
47              while(nextAddress!=0)
48              {
49                  System.out.print(" -> "+u.getInt(nextAddress));
50                  nextAddress=(u.getLong(nextAddress+Integer.SIZE));
51              }
52          }
53      }
54      public static void main(String[] args) {
55          LinkedList ll=new LinkedList();
56          for(int k=0; k<10000000; k++)
57          {
58              ll.add(k);
59          }
60          ll.traverse();
61      }
```

Output - Pointer (run) x

```
 9999940 -> 9999941 -> 9999942 -> 9999943 -> 9999944 -> 9999945 -> 9999946 -> 9999947 -> 9999948 -> 9999949
 -> 9999950 -> 9999951 -> 9999952 -> 9999953 -> 9999954 -> 9999955 -> 9999956 -> 9999957 -> 9999958 -> 9999
959 -> 9999960 -> 9999961 -> 9999962 -> 9999963 -> 9999964 -> 9999965 -> 9999966 -> 9999967 -> 9999968 -> 9
999969 -> 9999970 -> 9999971 -> 9999972 -> 9999973 -> 9999974 -> 9999975 -> 9999976 -> 9999977 -> 9999978 -
> 9999979 -> 9999980 -> 9999981 -> 9999982 -> 9999983 -> 9999984 -> 9999985 -> 9999986 -> 9999987 -> 999998
8 -> 9999989 -> 9999990 -> 9999991 -> 9999992 -> 9999993 -> 9999994 -> 9999995 -> 9999996 -> 9999997 -> 999
9998 -> 9999999BUILD SUCCESSFUL (total time: 3 minutes 10 seconds)
```

Figure 22: Output for Pointer's Code with n=10000000

6. EFFICIENT MEMORY MANAGEMENT

"A program which is unable to allocate a large amount of memory during normal execution could allocate that large amount of memory using Pointer code in Java."

Program:

```
/**
 * @Author Aatif Ahmad Khan
 * 12 October 2013
 */
package memory;
import java.lang.reflect.Field;
import sun.misc.Unsafe;
public class Memory {
    //main() function
    public static void main(String[] args) {
        try
        {
            System.out.println("Allocating 1GB Memory Space!");
            byte[] b=new byte[1073741824];
            for(int m=0; m<1073741824; m++)
            {
                b[m]='A';
                System.out.println(b[m]);
            }
        }
```

```java
        catch(OutOfMemoryError err)

        {

            System.out.println("Error: "+err);

            Unsafe u=getUnsafe();

            System.out.println("Allocating 1GB Using Pointers
in Java!");

            long address=u.allocateMemory(1073741824);

            for(int l=0; l<1073741824; l++)

            {

                u.putChar((address+l), 'A');

                char ch=u.getChar((address+l));

                System.out.println(ch);

            }

        }

    }

    //getUnsafe() function

    public static Unsafe getUnsafe()

    {

        boolean oh=false;

        Unsafe unsafe=null;

        try

        {

            Field f =
Unsafe.class.getDeclaredField("theUnsafe");

            f.setAccessible(true);

            oh=true;

            unsafe=(Unsafe)f.get(null);
```

```java
        }
        catch(Exception ex)
        {
            System.out.println("Exception: "+ex);
        }
        if(oh==false)
        {
            return null;
        }
        else
        {
            return unsafe;
        }
    }
}
```

End of Program

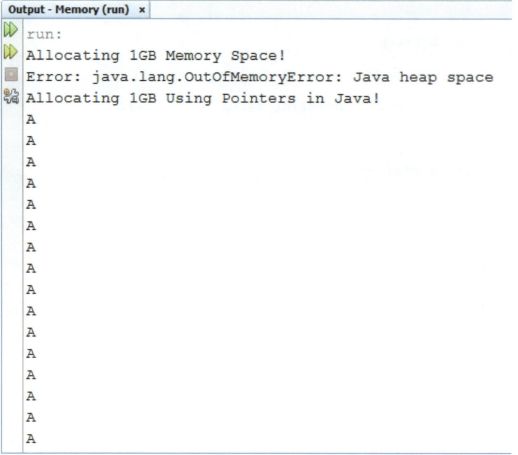

Figure 23: Output showing efficient memory allocation with use of Pointer's code

7. CONCLUSION AND FUTURE SCOPE

Pointers in Java could be securely used using Unsafe class. It results into no security flaw. On the other hand, advantages are many:

- Efficient and User Defined Memory Management
- Much Better Time Complexity

FUTURE SCOPE

Pointers could be used like in C/C++ with Pointer arithmetic as well. One could further extend the project to implement other structures using Pointers like Doubly Linked List, Tree etc.

8. REFERENCES

[1] "**Core Java**" Volume 1 – Fundamentals Eighth Edition by Cay S. Horstmann and Gary Cornell **Pearson**

[2] http://stackoverflow.com/questions/7934779/using-sun-misc-unsafe-to-get-address-of-java-array-items

[3] Unsafe class is private, so we can't instantiate it directly

[4] http://www.docjar.com/docs/api/sun/misc/Unsafe.html

[5] Size of int (or long) , in bytes, differs from machine to machine

APPENDIX 1: **CHAPTER 2 OF VOLUME 1**

Chapter 2: A simple Pointer program in Java

class PointersInJava{

    public static void main(String[] args)

    {

        //in place of "int a=11;" use this:

        PInt a=new PInt(11); //PInt stands for Pointer_Int

        long address=a.address; //storing address of 'a' in variable "address"

        //Now let us define a pointer (int pointer) and save address of 'a' into it

        Pointer ptr=new Pointer(address, int.class);

    }} //end of class

Output:

```
Start Page  x   PointersInJava.java  x
Source  History   
   1    package pointersinjava;
    □  import am.aatif.*;
   3    public class PointersInJava {
   4 □      public static void main(String[] args) {
   5            PInt a=new PInt(11);
   6            long address=a.address;
   7            Pointer ptr=new Pointer(address, int.class);
   8        }
   9    }
  10

Output - PointersInJava (run)  x
▷ run:
▷ int pointer created with value 17563312
   BUILD SUCCESSFUL (total time: 1 second)
```

APPENDIX 2: <u>CODE SNIPPETS FROM VOLUME 1</u>

```java
//Main Class

package pointersinjava;

import am.aatif.*;

public class PointersInJava {

        public static void main(String[] args) {

                //Int Type

                PInt a=new PInt(11);

                long intAddress=a.address;

                Pointer intptr=new Pointer(intAddress,
int.class);

                System.out.print("Value at address "+intAddress+"
is: ");

                intptr.valueAtAddress();

                //Byte Type

                PByte b=new PByte((byte)1);

                long byteAddress=b.address;

                Pointer byteptr=new Pointer(byteAddress,
byte.class);

                System.out.print("Value at address
"+byteAddress+" is: ");

                byteptr.valueAtAddress();

                //Char Type

                PChar c=new PChar('A');

                long charAddress=c.address;

                Pointer charptr=new Pointer(charAddress,
char.class);
```

```java
            System.out.print("Value at address
"+charAddress+" is: ");

            charptr.valueAtAddress();

            //Double type

            PDouble d=new PDouble(786);                long
doubleAddress=d.address;

            Pointer doubleptr=new Pointer(doubleAddress,
double.class);

            System.out.print("Value at address
"+doubleAddress+" is: ");

            doubleptr.valueAtAddress();

            //Short Type

            PShort s=new PShort((short)5);

            long shortAddress=s.address;

            Pointer shortptr=new Pointer(shortAddress,
short.class);

            System.out.print("Value at address
"+shortAddress+" is: ");

            shortptr.valueAtAddress();

            //Long Type

            PLong l=new PLong(1111110);

            long longAddress=l.address;

            Pointer longptr=new Pointer(longAddress,
long.class);

            System.out.print("Value at address
"+longAddress+" is: ");

            longptr.valueAtAddress();

    }

}

Output:
```

```java
//Package am.aatif contents:
//PInt.java
package am.aatif;
import java.lang.reflect.Field;
import sun.misc.Unsafe;
public class PInt {
        public int value;
        public long address;
        public static Unsafe getUnsafe()
        {
                boolean oh=false;
                Unsafe unsafe=null;
                try
                {
                        Field f =
Unsafe.class.getDeclaredField("theUnsafe");
                        f.setAccessible(true);
                        oh=true;
                        unsafe=(Unsafe)f.get(null);
                }
                catch(Exception ex)
                {
                        System.out.println("Exception: "+ex);
                }
                if(oh==false)
                {
                        return null;
```

```java
                    }            else
                    {
                        return unsafe;
                    }
        }
        public PInt(int value)
        {
            Unsafe unsafe=getUnsafe();
            this.value=value;
            this.address=unsafe.allocateMemory(4);
            unsafe.putInt(address, value);
        }
}
//PByte.java
package am.aatif;
import java.lang.reflect.Field;
import sun.misc.Unsafe;
public class PByte {
        public byte value;
        public long address;
        public static Unsafe getUnsafe()
        {
            boolean oh=false;
            Unsafe unsafe=null;
            try
            {
```

```
                Field f =
Unsafe.class.getDeclaredField("theUnsafe");
f.setAccessible(true);

                oh=true;

                unsafe=(Unsafe)f.get(null);

        }

        catch(Exception ex)

        {

                System.out.println("Exception: "+ex);

        }

        if(oh==false)

        {

                return null;

        }

        else

        {

                return unsafe;

        }

    }

    public PByte(byte value)

    {

        Unsafe unsafe=getUnsafe();

        this.value=value;

        this.address=unsafe.allocateMemory(1);

        unsafe.putByte(address, value);

    }

}
```

```java
//PChar.java
package am.aatif;
import java.lang.reflect.Field;
import sun.misc.Unsafe;
public class PChar {
        public char value;
        public long address;
        public static Unsafe getUnsafe()
        {
                boolean oh=false;
                Unsafe unsafe=null;
                try
                {
                        Field f =
Unsafe.class.getDeclaredField("theUnsafe");
                        f.setAccessible(true);
                        oh=true;
                        unsafe=(Unsafe)f.get(null);
                }
                catch(Exception ex)
                {
                        System.out.println("Exception: "+ex);
                }
                if(oh==false)
                {
                        return null;
```

```java
            }
            else                {
                    return unsafe;
            }
        }
        public PChar(char value)
        {
                Unsafe unsafe=getUnsafe();
                this.value=value;
                this.address=unsafe.allocateMemory(2);
                unsafe.putChar(address, value);
        }
}
//PDouble.java
package am.aatif;
import java.lang.reflect.Field;
import sun.misc.Unsafe;
public class PDouble {
        public double value;
        public long address;
        public static Unsafe getUnsafe()
        {
                boolean oh=false;
                Unsafe unsafe=null;
                try
                {
```

```java
                Field f =
Unsafe.class.getDeclaredField("theUnsafe");

                f.setAccessible(true);
oh=true;

                unsafe=(Unsafe)f.get(null);
        }
        catch(Exception ex)
        {
                System.out.println("Exception: "+ex);
        }
        if(oh==false)
        {
                return null;
        }
        else
        {
                return unsafe;
        }
    }
    public PDouble(double value)
    {
        Unsafe unsafe=getUnsafe();
        this.value=value;
        this.address=unsafe.allocateMemory(16);
        unsafe.putDouble(address, value);
    }
}
```

```java
//PShort.java
package am.aatif;
import java.lang.reflect.Field;
import sun.misc.Unsafe;
public class PShort {
        public short value;
        public long address;
        public static Unsafe getUnsafe()
        {
                boolean oh=false;
                Unsafe unsafe=null;
                try
                {
                        Field f =
Unsafe.class.getDeclaredField("theUnsafe");
                        f.setAccessible(true);
                        oh=true;
                        unsafe=(Unsafe)f.get(null);
                }
                catch(Exception ex)
                {
                        System.out.println("Exception: "+ex);
                }
                if(oh==false)
                {
```

```java
                return null;
            }
            else                {
                return unsafe;
            }
        }
        public PShort(short value)
        {
            Unsafe unsafe=getUnsafe();
            this.value=value;
            this.address=unsafe.allocateMemory(2);
            unsafe.putShort(address, value);
        }
}
//PLong.java
package am.aatif;
import java.lang.reflect.Field;
import sun.misc.Unsafe;
public class PLong {
    public long value;
    public long address;
    public static Unsafe getUnsafe()
    {
        boolean oh=false;
        Unsafe unsafe=null;
        try
        {
```

```java
                Field f =
Unsafe.class.getDeclaredField("theUnsafe");

                f.setAccessible(true);
oh=true;

                unsafe=(Unsafe)f.get(null);
        }
        catch(Exception ex)
        {
                System.out.println("Exception: "+ex);
        }
        if(oh==false)
        {
                return null;
        }
        else
        {
                return unsafe;
        }
    }
    public PLong(long value)
    {
        Unsafe unsafe=getUnsafe();
        this.value=value;
        this.address=unsafe.allocateMemory(8);
        unsafe.putLong(address, value);
    }
}
```

```java
//Pointer.java
package am.aatif;

import java.lang.reflect.Field;

import sun.misc.Unsafe;

public class Pointer {

    public Class type;

    public long value;

    public Pointer(long value, Class type)

    {

        this.value=value;

        this.type=type;

        System.out.println(type+" pointer created with value
"+value);

    }

    public static Unsafe getUnsafe()

    {

        boolean oh=false;

        Unsafe unsafe=null;

        try

        {

            Field f =
Unsafe.class.getDeclaredField("theUnsafe");

            f.setAccessible(true);

            oh=true;

            unsafe=(Unsafe)f.get(null);
```

```java
        }
        catch(Exception ex)
        {
            System.out.println("Exception: "+ex);          }
        if(oh==false)
        {
            return null;
        }
        else
        {
            return unsafe;
        }
    }
    public void valueAtAddress()
    {
        Unsafe unsafe=getUnsafe();
        if(this.type==int.class)
        {
            System.out.println(unsafe.getInt(value));
        }
        else if(this.type==byte.class)
        {
            System.out.println(unsafe.getByte(value));
        }
        else if(this.type==char.class)
        {
            System.out.println(unsafe.getChar(value));
```

```java
        }
        else if(this.type==long.class)
        {
System.out.println(unsafe.getLong(value));
        }
        else if(this.type==short.class)
        {
            System.out.println(unsafe.getShort(value));
        }
        else if(this.type==double.class)
        {
            System.out.println(unsafe.getDouble(value));
        }
    }
}
//End of Code
```

APPENDIX 3: <u>GETUNSAFE() METHOD CODE</u>

```java
public static Unsafe getUnsafe()
    {
            boolean oh=false;
            Unsafe unsafe=null;
            try
            {
                Field f =
Unsafe.class.getDeclaredField("theUnsafe");
                f.setAccessible(true);
                oh=true;
                unsafe=(Unsafe)f.get(null);
            }
            catch(Exception ex)
            { System.out.println("Exception: "+ex);
}
            if(oh==false)
            { return null;  }
            else
            { return unsafe;    }
    }
```